THE SEVEN WONDERS
OF THE MODERN WORLD

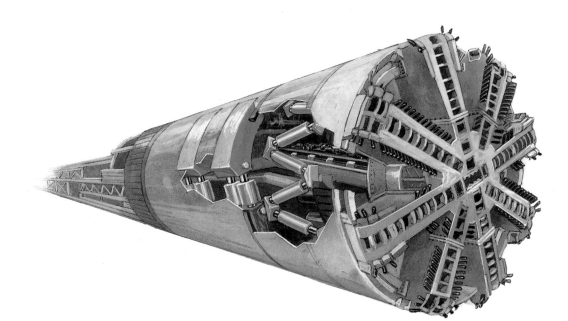

Reg Cox & Neil Morris

Belitha Press

16

8

16

24

28

INTRODUCTION

Over 2000 years ago, a Greek poet wrote about some of the amazing buildings and statues of his time. His list of the Seven Wonders of the Ancient World has survived to this day. But what would he choose to include in his list if he were alive now?

The seven wonders of the modern world chosen for this book are all outstanding examples of human achievement. The selection includes two amazing buildings, a dam, the world's longest undersea tunnel,

and an airport on a man-made island. Then there is the fastest form of modern passenger transport – a supersonic aircraft. And the list is completed by a space-age launch site from which human beings are able to leave their own planet and explore beyond it. All these wonders tell us a great deal about ourselves and the way in which we live in the modern world. Some of them have brought problems along with their benefits. But they are all truly wonders of modern design, engineering and construction.

CONTENTS

Words in bold are explained in
the glossary on page 32.

20

12

4

SYDNEY OPERA HOUSE

This unusual modern building is one of the most famous sights of Australia. The Opera House was built in Australia's oldest and biggest city, overlooking a natural deep-water harbour. It is surrounded on three sides by water, and its roofs were specially designed to look like giant sails.

DESIGN COMPETITION
In the early 1950s an international competition was held to design a new arts centre in Sydney. The site chosen was Bennelong Point, a narrow piece of land jutting out into the harbour.

THE WINNER
The winner was a Danish **architect** called Jørn Utzon. The judges thought that his entry was the most imaginative. It was inspired by sails in the harbour, and by **Aztec** and **Maya** temples. But his amazing construction was not easy to build.

BUILDING WORK BEGINS
Work began on the **foundations** in 1959, and it took four years to complete the base of the building. Next came the most challenging part of the whole construction – the shell roof. Nothing like this had ever been built before.

THE SHELL ROOF

The shells that form the roof make this building different from any other in the world. They are made of over 2000 **prefabricated** concrete sections, held together by 350 kilometres of steel cable. The shells are covered with over a million **ceramic** tiles. The glossy white and buff-coloured tiles create a pattern that glints in the sunlight.

UTZON RESIGNS

The builders disagreed on how to build the roof and the original design had to be adapted. In 1966 Jørn Utzon resigned from the project. Four Australian architects took over, and the roof was finished a year later. It took another six years to make everything ready inside the building.

FOUR HALLS

The Sydney Opera House was officially opened by Queen Elizabeth II in October 1973. Inside the centre, there are four main performing halls. The largest is the Concert Hall, which seats over 2600 people. Above the Concert Hall, the tip of the largest shell towers 67 metres above the harbour. The Opera Theatre itself is smaller, with over 1500 seats. The other main halls are the Drama Theatre and the Playhouse.

LASTING POPULARITY

In the first 20 years after it opened, the Opera House was visited by 36 million people – over twice the population of Australia. More than 2500 performances are held there each year, of opera, pop concerts, plays and other events.

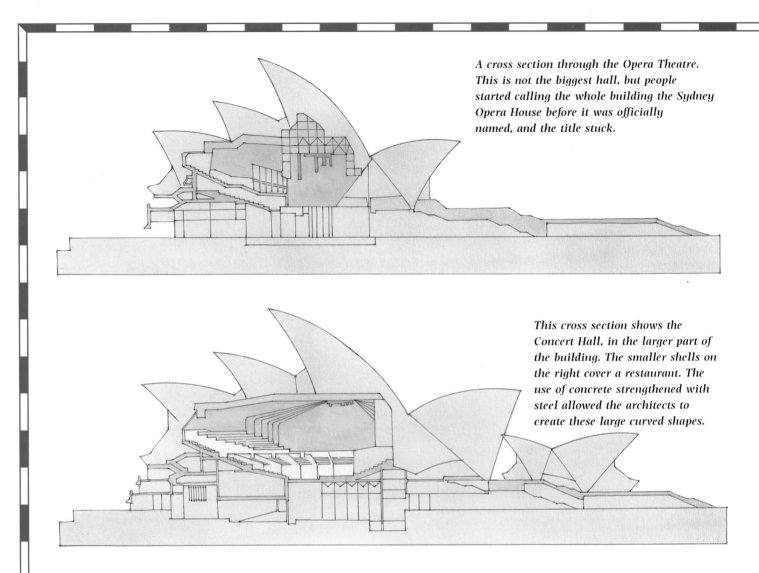

A cross section through the Opera Theatre. This is not the biggest hall, but people started calling the whole building the Sydney Opera House before it was officially named, and the title stuck.

This cross section shows the Concert Hall, in the larger part of the building. The smaller shells on the right cover a restaurant. The use of concrete strengthened with steel allowed the architects to create these large curved shapes.

A photo (left) of the Opera House being built. The building is 185 metres long and 120 metres across at its widest point.

The Curtain of the Sun, in the Opera Theatre, is made of Australian wool. It is over 8 metres high and almost 16 metres wide.

A performance in the Concert Hall (left). Behind the stage is the grand organ, which has 10 500 pipes. This is the world's largest mechanical organ.

The mouths of the shell roof (right) contain 2000 panes of tinted glass. They are double thickness to keep out noise.

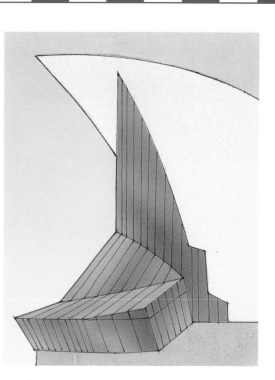

Plastic rings or 'clouds' (below) hang above the orchestra platform. They help to improve the quality of sound.

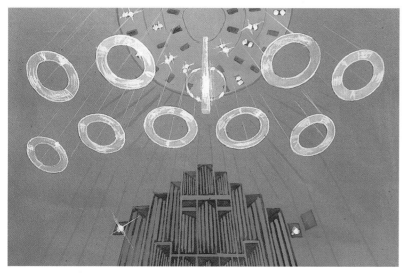

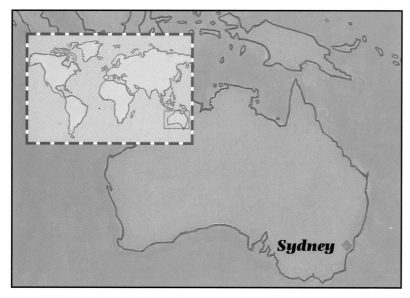

Sydney

The roof tiles were made in Sweden. They were arranged in curved sections before being bolted to the roof.

CHANNEL TUNNEL

The world's longest undersea tunnel runs under the English Channel, between England and France. It is an amazing engineering achievement. The tunnel, sometimes called the Chunnel, is just over 50 kilometres long and runs for 38 kilometres under the sea bed. The Seikan Tunnel in Japan is slightly longer, but runs under more land and less sea. The Channel Tunnel was opened in 1994 as part of an up-to-date transport system linking Britain with the **Continent**.

CONTINENTAL LINK

For the last 200 years, engineers have made many suggestions for a cross-Channel link. A tunnel was first proposed in 1802, and a Channel Tunnel Committee was formed as long ago as 1872. Some engineers have even considered building a bridge across the Channel. But it was not until 1985 that the British and French governments asked companies to draw up serious plans for a tunnel. A year later they chose the best of the nine schemes they received.

DIGGING THE TUNNEL

The Chunnel is, in fact, three tunnels – two rail tunnels and a smaller **service tunnel**. Digging began from the English side in December 1987, and from the French side three months later. Huge machines with revolving cutting heads took a month to dig each kilometre. Altogether the tunnelling took three years.

BREAKTHROUGH

The tunnels were bored at an average depth of 45 metres beneath the sea bed. When the two halves of the service tunnel were just 100 metres apart, a small tunnel was dug by hand to connect them. Workers broke through at the end of 1990. The breakthroughs of the two rail tunnels took place on 22 May and 28 June 1991.

READY FOR USE

Seven months later all three tunnels were connected, ready to be cleaned up and have railway tracks laid. At the same time, engineers were working on the rail **terminals** at Folkestone, in England, and near Calais in France. The Channel Tunnel was opened by Queen Elizabeth II and President Mitterrand on 6 May 1994.

SHUTTLE SERVICE

Cars, coaches and lorries use the tunnel's shuttle service like a moving motorway. They drive on to a carriage at one end, and off at the other after a 35-minute trip. Electric locomotives drive the shuttles at up to 160 kilometres an hour. Special high-speed trains also carry passengers non-stop between London, Paris and Brussels.

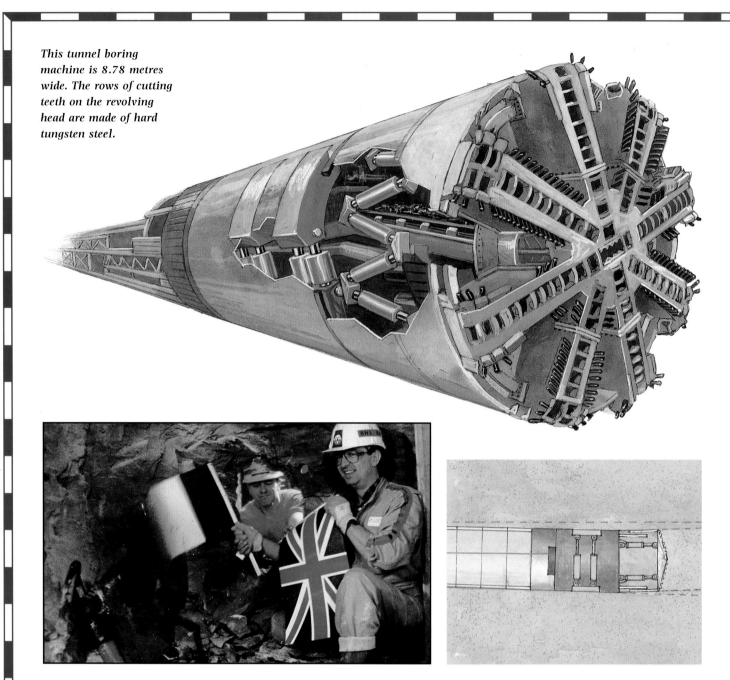

This tunnel boring machine is 8.78 metres wide. The rows of cutting teeth on the revolving head are made of hard tungsten steel.

French and English tunnellers broke through to meet each other beneath the Channel on 1 December 1990, after three years' work.

Laser beams and computers guided the boring machines along a precise path.

The engineers tunnelled through a layer of soft rock called chalk marl. This waterproof rock is a mixture of chalk and clay. It runs almost right across the Channel.

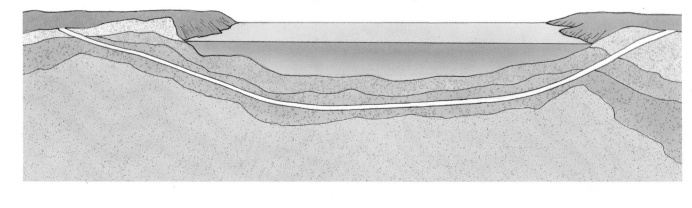

There are two cross-over points where trains can change track if one tunnel is closed. Huge sliding doors open to allow the cross-over.

Service tunnel

Sliding door

The Tunnel was opened for use in 1994. Cars drive down the loading ramp towards the boarding platform and the waiting train.

This cutaway shows cars driving on to a shuttle's loading wagon. Drivers and passengers stay with their car during the journey.

Channel Tunnel

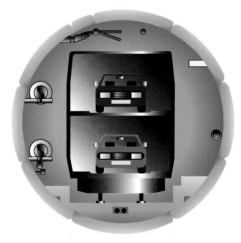

This cross section through a tunnel shows a passenger vehicle shuttle. They carry cars, coaches and motorcycles. Freight shuttles carry lorries.

KANSAI AIRPORT

Kansai International Airport, in Osaka Bay, Japan, is the world's first **offshore** airport. It was completed in 1994. This spectacular airport has a **futuristic** steel and glass terminal building, and stands on an entirely man-made island. The terminal is 1.7 kilometres long, which makes it one of the world's longest buildings. Engineers used the most up-to-date technology in creating the island and its airport.

OFFSHORE AIRPORT

Why build an airport in the sea? One reason is that there is an increasing problem finding space to build large airports near cities. Another reason is to reduce noise disturbance. The new Kansai Airport lies 5 kilometres off the coast of Honshu, Japan's largest island. Aircraft take off and land at Kansai over the sea, so the airport can stay open 24 hours a day without disturbing people.

MAN-MADE ISLAND

Once the idea for a new island had been discussed, engineers drew up plans to create an island 4 kilometres long and 1.25 kilometres wide. At first they considered building a floating island, but this would have cost more and been less stable. The island took five years to construct.

HOW TO BUILD AN ISLAND

First sand and earth were piled onto the sea bed, 20 metres deep in Osaka Bay. Then crushed rock was carried to the site by huge barges and dumped on top. The weight of the rock gradually squeezed water out of the sea bed, creating a solid foundation. Computers and space **satellites** were used to make sure the barges and their loads were in the right place. Finally, a large steel boundary was sunk all around the edge of the rectangular island.

PRIZE-WINNING DESIGN

A competition was held to find an architect to design the airport. The winner was Renzo Piano, one of the architects of the famous Pompidou Centre in Paris. Building work started on the airport even before the island was finished.

Piano's company decided to build a 1700 metre long terminal in which passengers could move easily from one end to the other, from the entrance to their waiting plane. The central part is a four-storey building with a huge, curved roof designed to look like an aircraft wing. Computers constantly **monitor** the building's 900 columns, so that their height can be slightly adjusted. This is important, because the island is still settling and will go on sinking slightly for some years.

TRANSPORT NETWORK

The airport island is connected to the mainland by a two-level bridge, with railway lines on the lower level and a road on top. Kansai has only one runway, but can handle 160 000 flights and 25 million passengers each year. In time, the world's most amazing airport may be made even bigger, and other islands may be built near to it.

Curved steel and glass form the side of Kansai's passenger terminal. The wing shape looks incredible from the ground and the air.

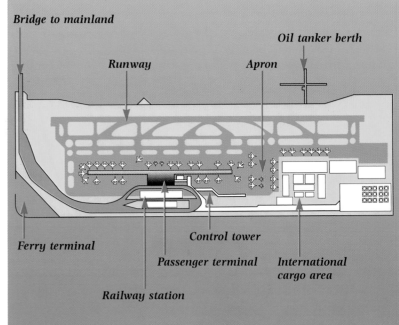

Bridge to mainland

Runway

Oil tanker berth

Apron

Ferry terminal

Control tower

Passenger terminal

International cargo area

Railway station

A plan of the airport and its island. The runway is 3500 metres long and 60 metres wide. High-speed boats reach the ferry terminal from the port of Kobe in 30 minutes.

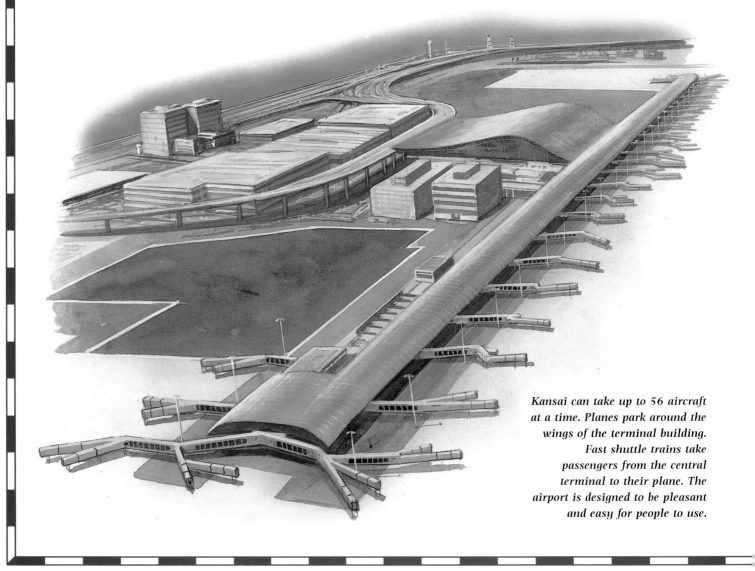

Kansai can take up to 56 aircraft at a time. Planes park around the wings of the terminal building. Fast shuttle trains take passengers from the central terminal to their plane. The airport is designed to be pleasant and easy for people to use.

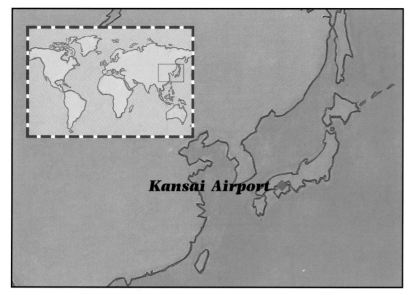

Kansai Airport

Passengers wait in one of the boarding wings. The terminal is constructed to withstand high winds, storms and earthquakes.

How the island grew, from the first surrounding wall (below left), through a half-submerged stage to a complete island (right).

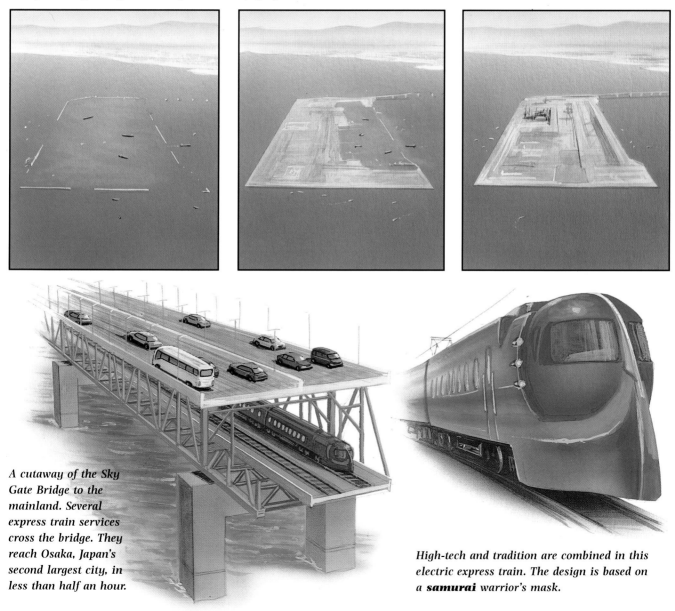

A cutaway of the Sky Gate Bridge to the mainland. Several express train services cross the bridge. They reach Osaka, Japan's second largest city, in less than half an hour.

High-tech and tradition are combined in this electric express train. The design is based on a **samurai** warrior's mask.

CONCORDE

oncorde is the world's only **supersonic** passenger aircraft. It has been flying for many years, but the sight of a Concorde taking off or landing is still an exciting one. When it was developed, this sleek aircraft revolutionized air transport, and it continues to be a symbol of speed and luxury.

FLYING AT THE SPEED OF SOUND
On the ground, sound travels at a speed of 1225 kilometres an hour. The speed of sound in the air is slightly slower – pilots call it Mach 1. Twice the speed of sound is Mach 2. By the 1940s, the fastest planes were almost flying at Mach 1. Then in 1947 a US Air Force research plane broke the **sound barrier**.

SUPERSONIC PROBLEMS
Pilots noticed that when planes flew at supersonic speeds they met huge shock waves, which acted like a barrier. The waves caused loud noises like thunder, called sonic booms. The planes also became dangerously hot. Despite such problems, engineers set about designing supersonic aircraft that could withstand these effects.

INTERNATIONAL COOPERATION
In the 1950s British and French engineers worked separately on developing a supersonic airliner. Then in 1962 the British Aircraft Corporation and French Aérospatiale joined forces. They worked together with Rolls-Royce and SNECMA, who manufactured jet engines.

NAMING THE PLANE

The companies called the plane they were developing Concorde, which means harmony between nations. After seven years' work, the end product was a narrow, 100-seat aircraft with swept-back wings and a nose section that could be lowered when taking off and landing.

TAKING OFF

Two Concordes were built in each of the two countries. The first took off at Toulouse, in France, on 2 March 1969. Engineers and pilots spent 5000 flying hours testing the plane, making it the most tested aircraft in history. Concorde finally entered service in 1976 with British Airways and Air France. Today each airline has a fleet of seven Concordes. Only 16 production models have ever been built, with two remaining at the **development bases**.

FUTURISTIC TECHNOLOGY

Concorde is 62.1 metres long, with a wingspan of 25.5 metres. It cruises at a height of up to 18 300 metres at Mach 2 – faster than some rifle bullets. It mainly flies from London and Paris to New York. Its New York to London record, set in 1990, is 2 hours and 54 minutes – less than three hours to cross the Atlantic Ocean. The aircraft follow routes that allow their sonic booms to take place over the sea.

THE END OF CONCORDE

Although Concorde is, technologically, a modern wonder, it is not a great commercial success. Eventually the whole fleet will be grounded. The planes now being developed are much larger and can fly vast distances without having to refuel. They can carry more passengers and cargo, and cause less noise pollution.

BRITISH AIRWAYS

An early Concorde being built. Eight production aircraft were put together at Filton, in the west of England, and eight at Toulouse, in southern France (see map, below).

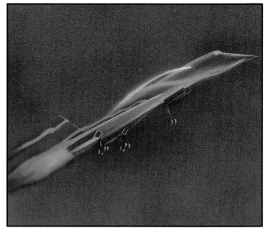

New aircraft designs are tested by placing a model of the aircraft in a tunnel, through which a controlled airstream flows. Wind tunnels with supersonic airstreams were used to test Concorde's shape. Its pointed **fuselage** and swept-back, or delta, wings make it streamlined.

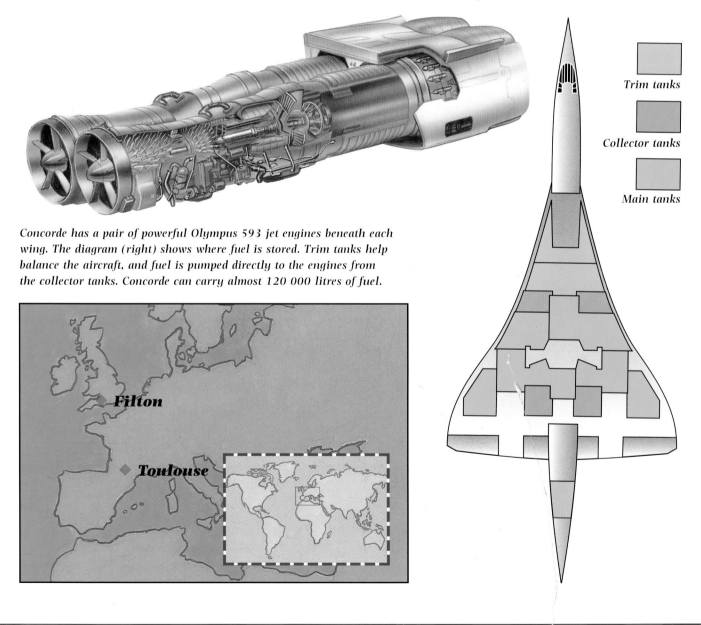

Concorde has a pair of powerful Olympus 593 jet engines beneath each wing. The diagram (right) shows where fuel is stored. Trim tanks help balance the aircraft, and fuel is pumped directly to the engines from the collector tanks. Concorde can carry almost 120 000 litres of fuel.

Trim tanks

Collector tanks

Main tanks

Filton

Toulouse

Cabin indicators tell passengers how fast they are flying. At Concorde's cruising height, Mach 2 (twice the speed of sound) is 2156 kilometres per hour.

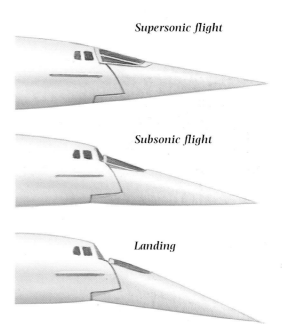

Supersonic flight

Subsonic flight

Landing

In supersonic flight, Concorde's nose points straight forward. At slower speeds, it can be lowered. When the aircraft is landing, the adjustable nose goes right down so that the pilot has a good view of the runway.

The cutaway picture (above) shows two rows of double seats in the passenger cabin. This is much narrower than other modern aircraft. Weather radar is installed in the nose section. When Concorde takes off, it uses the same amount of thrust as 3000 cars all accelerating at the same time.

Pilot and co-pilot on the flight deck. A flight engineer sits behind them, and there are six cabin crew members on Concorde.

ASWAN HIGH DAM

This huge dam was a vast and ambitious project. It was built to hold back the waters of the world's longest river, the Nile. The dam has helped to create a steady flow of water all year round, and provides electricity for the country's factories and towns.

NILE FLOODS
Since ancient times, the River Nile has flooded every year. The floods spread fertile mud over the land, helping farmers to grow their crops. But often big floods destroyed homes and farmland. At other times of the year there was drought.

CONTROLLING THE NILE
In 1902 engineers built a dam just south of Aswan to control the floods. This dam was made higher in 1912 and again in 1933. But this first Aswan Dam was still not enough to control the Nile fully.

Building work started on the Aswan High Dam in 1960. The dam is made of earth and granite **rock-fill**, with a core of clay and cement. It is over 3.6 kilometres wide, 111 metres high and 40 metres thick at the top. At its base on the river bed, it is a massive 925 metres thick. The dam took ten years to build.

LAKE NASSER

Aswan High Dam was officially opened in 1971. During the rainy season, the dam holds back the Nile's rising waters. As the waters rose behind the dam, they gradually formed a **reservoir** more than 500 kilometres long. The new reservoir was called Lake Nasser after the Egyptian president.

CREATING THE LAKE

Around 50 000 people had to leave their homes to make way for the reservoir. They were taken to a new farming region 50 kilometres north of Aswan. Several ancient temples and islands were flooded, but some were rescued. In a huge-scale operation, the temples of Ramses II and Nefertari were cut into 30-tonne blocks and put together again, piece by piece, on hills overlooking the river. This difficult work took four years. Other small temples were also moved from an island in the Nile which was to be totally submerged.

BENEFITS

The water stored in Lake Nasser is used to **irrigate** farmland during dry periods and throughout the year. More crops can now be grown every year, producing more food to feed the growing population. As the water pours through the dam, it also drives **turbines**, which generate half of Egypt's electricity.

PROBLEMS

This human attempt to control nature has brought many problems as well as benefits. The dam stops fertile mud from moving downstream, so that farmers have to use more chemicals to fertilize their land. Since the dam was built, there has also been an increase in a disease carried by tiny worms in the Nile's water snails. Yearly floods used to keep the numbers of snails down. A rise in the **water table** has also brought salts to the surface, which make the land infertile.

Since Roman times, Egyptians have used the lines on this 'nilometer' to tell the depth of the Nile's annual flood. It is on the river's Elephantine Island, near Aswan.

Building the High Dam was a huge project. It was designed in Germany and built with the help of the Soviet Union.

*A cross section through the huge complex of the dam. The Nile's water flows from left to right. It is diverted through a channel to drive a **generator** on the other side of the dam.*

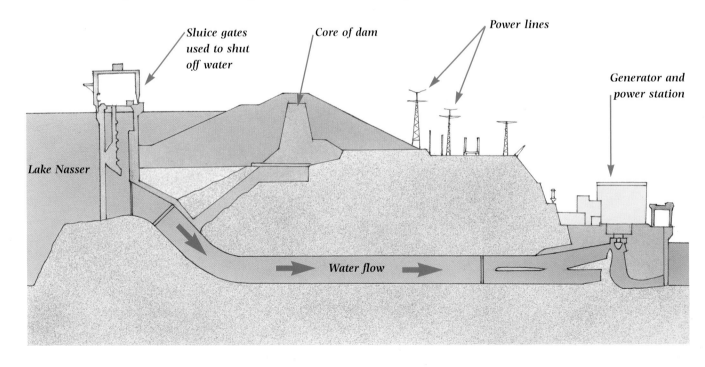

Sluice gates used to shut off water

Core of dam

Power lines

Generator and power station

Lake Nasser

Water flow

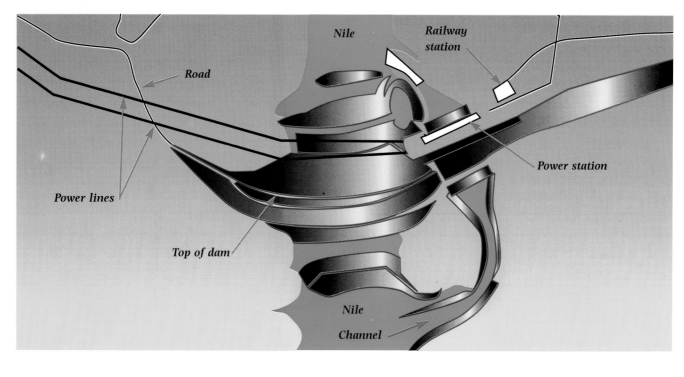

The temple of Ramses II at Abu Simbel was built over 3000 years ago. Workers cut the temple into blocks and moved it to a specially-built mountain, to save it from flooding.

Temples from the flooded island of Philae, 6 kilometres north of the High Dam, were moved to nearby Agilkia Island (right).

In this plan of the High Dam area, the Nile flows from the bottom. A four-lane road runs across the top of the dam.

Aswan High Dam

Nile

Railway station

Road

Power station

Power lines

Top of dam

Nile

Channel

SEARS TOWER

This 110-storey skyscraper in Chicago, USA, is the tallest building in the world. Sears Tower is 443 metres high, which is over 60 metres taller than the Empire State Building in New York City. The tower was originally built as the national headquarters of the Sears, Roebuck Company.

THE BEGINNING

People generally agree that the skyscraper was invented in Chicago, the third largest city in the USA. In 1871 a fire destroyed a third of the city, and architects set about rebuilding it. By this time, steel was being mass produced and, in 1852, Elisha Otis had invented the lift. New buildings could safely and practically be made much taller. The first high-rise building appeared in the city in 1882. This was the Home Insurance Company Building. It was the first building to have a skeleton structure made entirely of steel and iron. It had ten floors – a hundred fewer than Sears Tower, built 90 years later.

BUILDING UPWARDS

As the demand for land in city centres grew, people needed to build fast and economically. Skyscrapers were the perfect solution. With new materials and technology, the design of skyscrapers was gradually improved and perfected. Steel **girders** were used in different ways to make a strong framework. Some buildings were made of tall steel tubes, designed to withstand the winds that blow around the top levels. Inside the tubes, individual floors and rooms are rigid so that people can live and work safely and comfortably.

In 1985 a four-storey hall was built at the base of Sears Tower, to give extra space. There are also shops and restaurants in the building.

THE ULTIMATE SKYSCRAPER

It took 2400 workers three years to build Sears Tower, which was finished in 1973. The tower's unique framework is made up of nine square tubes, which form a large square at the base. This rests on concrete, rock-filled **shafts** that are securely fitted into the solid rock beneath. The nine **welded** steel tubes rise 50 floors up. Then the building starts to narrow. Seven tubes continue on up to the 66th floor. Then five rise on to the 90th floor, leaving just two tubes to form the top 20 floors. Two television antennae take the building's total height to 520 metres – over half a kilometre. The amount of steel used to build the framework was enough to make more than 52 000 cars.

OPERATING THE BUILDING

This huge building has over 418 000 square metres of space. That's more than 57 football pitches. The Tower has 104 high-speed lifts, which divide the building into three separate zones and make it easier for people to find their way around. The fireproofed frame is covered in a skin made of black **aluminium** and more than 16 000 bronze-tinted glass windows. Six automatic window-washing machines clean the whole of the building eight times a year.

TOURIST ATTRACTION

About 1.5 million tourists visit Sears Tower each year. Two express lifts take them up to the 103rd floor in just over a minute. From the tower's Skydeck, visitors have spectacular, panoramic views of Chicago. In the building's lobby there is an enormous 'wallmobile' by the famous sculptor Alexander Calder.

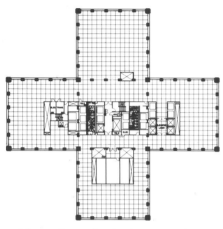

Two steel tubes form the top stage of the tower.
Each tube is 23 metres square.

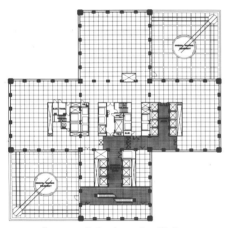

Viewed from above, the third stage makes
up a cross shape of five tubes.

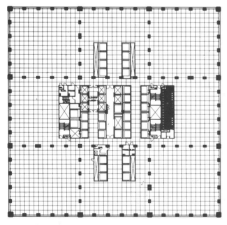

The second stage of the 'step-back' design
has seven tubes that rise for 65 metres.

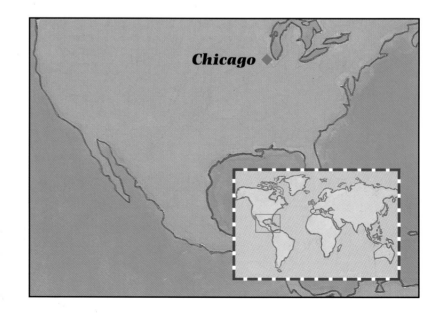

Each side of the tower's base, made up of nine
tubes, is 69 metres long. The total structure
weighs over 200 500 tonnes.

Sears Tower makes the high-rise buildings around it look small.
It is designed to sway up to 90 centimetres at the top in strong winds.

Chicago ◆

The view from the Skydeck, 412 metres up. On a clear day, visitors can see over 80 kilometres. This gives a view of four states – Illinois, Indiana, Michigan and Wisconsin.

The building's steel frame (above) was put together in sections. Then these were welded and bolted in place at the site.

During construction, up to eight floors were added to the building every month.

Below are some of the world's tallest structures. The 553-metre CN Tower is the tallest free-standing structure. Yokohama has the tallest lighthouse.

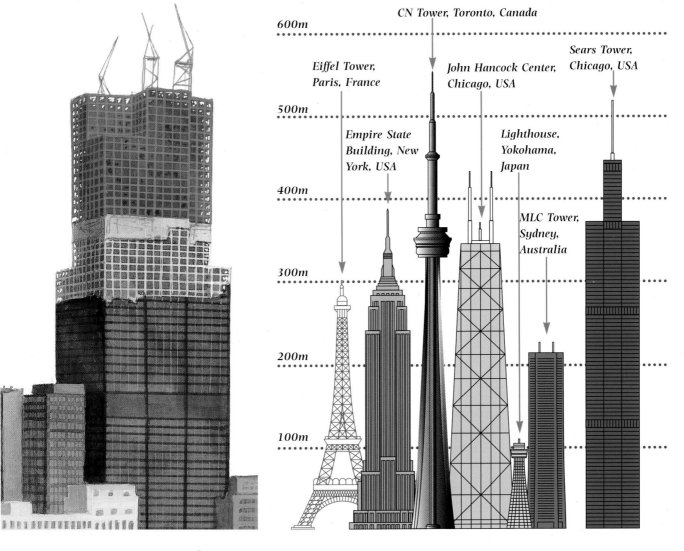

CN Tower, Toronto, Canada

600m

Eiffel Tower, Paris, France

John Hancock Center, Chicago, USA

Sears Tower, Chicago, USA

500m

Empire State Building, New York, USA

Lighthouse, Yokohama, Japan

400m

MLC Tower, Sydney, Australia

300m

200m

100m

KENNEDY SPACE CENTER

The Kennedy Space Center is probably best known as the launch site of the Apollo space programme, which sent people to the Moon in the 1960s and 1970s. Today, the Center is both a working site and a tourist attraction. Visitors can see an exhibition of space rockets and visit the **assembly areas** and the space shuttle launch pads on Cape Canaveral. The cape, on the Atlantic coast of Florida, was the starting point for many of the most exciting scientific explorations made this century.

CAPE CANAVERAL

The site was originally a US Air Force base and missile test centre. It was used to launch the first US satellite in 1958. Then on 5 May 1961 Alan Shepard blasted off in a Mercury spacecraft, to become the first American in space. Three weeks later, President Kennedy announced the Apollo programme, to build a spacecraft that could land men on the Moon by 1970. After the President's death in 1963, the site was renamed the John F. Kennedy Space Center.

SPACECRAFT ASSEMBLY

The Apollo spacecraft that travelled to the Moon were launched by powerful Saturn rockets. The rockets were put together in a huge, 160 metre high building that could hold four Saturn rockets at a time. The spacecraft and rockets then had to be moved over 5 kilometres to the launch pad. The whole assembly weighed over 5000 tonnes and was carried on a massive vehicle called a crawler-transporter. The crawler is 40 metres long, 35 metres wide and moves at a top speed of 1.6 kilometres an hour.

THE FIRST MAN ON THE MOON

The first Apollo mission was due to be launched in 1967, but disaster struck at the Space Center. During a routine countdown test, fire suddenly swept through the space capsule at the tip of the rocket, and the three astronauts on board were killed. The Apollo programme was changed to allow more unmanned test flights. Then on 16 July 1969, a giant Saturn rocket blasted off from launch pad 39, sending Apollo 11 astronauts on their journey into space. Four days later, Neil Armstrong was the first human being to set foot on the surface of the Moon.

THE SPACE SHUTTLE

During the 1970s, the huge expense of the Apollo Moon programme led to the development of a new type of space vehicle – the space shuttle. The shuttle looked more like an aeroplane than a moon rocket and, unlike a rocket, it could be used time and time again. A fixed launch tower was placed at launch pad 39, ready for the first shuttle flight in 1981. A runway, 4572 metres long, was also built, so that shuttles could land back at the Space Center after each mission.

A NEW FRONTIER

By 1986 NASA had launched 24 successful shuttle missions. But then Shuttle Challenger exploded after take-off and all seven astronauts were killed. Over two years passed before the next shuttle lifted off in September 1988. Since then a large number of scientific and commercial missions have been launched from Kennedy Space Center in pursuit of the dream of living and working in space.

The mission emblem of Apollo 11 (above). Its lunar module was named the Eagle.

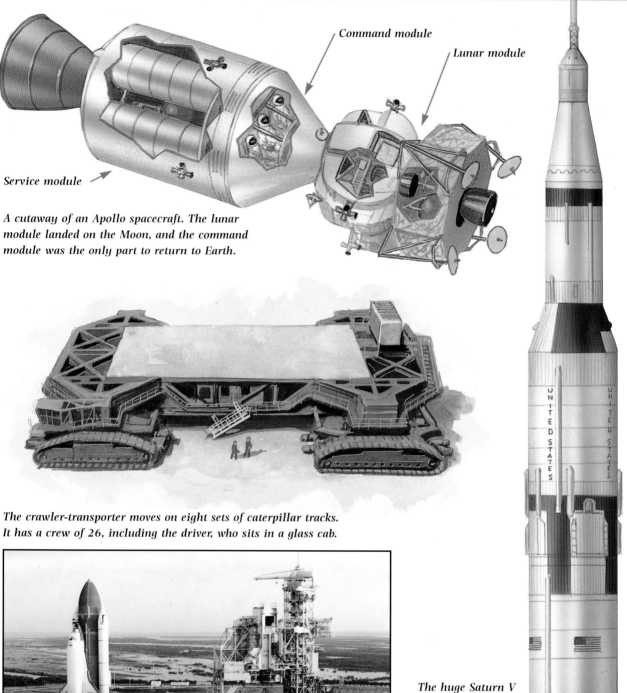

Command module

Lunar module

Service module

A cutaway of an Apollo spacecraft. The lunar module landed on the Moon, and the command module was the only part to return to Earth.

The crawler-transporter moves on eight sets of caterpillar tracks. It has a crew of 26, including the driver, who sits in a glass cab.

The space shuttle Discovery travels on the crawler-transporter to its launch pad ready for its seventh space flight, in 1988.

The huge Saturn V rocket that sent astronauts to the Moon. It was 111 metres long. The Apollo spacecraft is at the top, just beneath the pointed emergency escape rocket.

Inside the Center's assembly building, Discovery is already attached to its enormous, empty fuel tank.

A shuttle's 47 metre long external tank is filled with fuel on the launch pad. The two rocket boosters at the sides help the shuttle blast off from the Space Center.

Using a manned manoeuvring unit, an astronaut can leave the shuttle and move about in space. The MMU is powered by tiny gas jets.

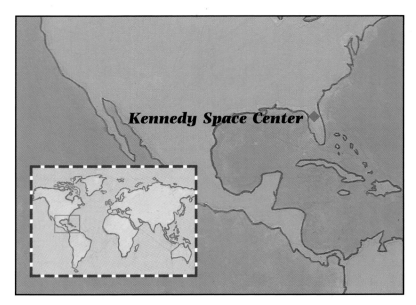

Kennedy Space Center

GLOSSARY

aluminium: a light metal that does not rust.

architect: a person who designs buildings.

assembly area: where a structure is put together.

Aztec: built by the Aztecs, an Indian people of Mexico.

ceramic: made of hardened, heated clay.

Continent: the mainland of Europe (a continent is a huge land mass).

development base: the place where an aircraft is created and built.

foundations: the underground base that supports a building.

fuselage: the main body of an aircraft.

futuristic: designed in a very modern way.

generator: a machine that turns one form of energy, such as the power of water, into electricity.

girder: a large beam.

irrigate: to water (land) using canals and ditches.

Maya: built by the Maya, an Indian people of Mexico and Central America.

monitor: to check and control.

offshore: built on an island in the sea.

prefabricated: made earlier in a factory.

reservoir: a lake used to collect and store water.

rock-fill: material used to fill a hole and raise the level of the ground.

samurai: powerful Japanese warriors.

satellite: a device that circles the Earth in space and sends back information.

service tunnel: a tunnel used for carrying equipment and making repairs.

shaft: a long deep hole.

sound barrier: the speed of sound. It used to be thought of as a barrier to planes.

supersonic: able to fly faster than the speed of sound.

terminal: a station at the beginning and end of a railway line.

turbine: a machine with blades that are turned by moving water.

water table: the underground level where rocks are full of water.

weld: to join by heating and hammering.

INDEX

This edition published in 2002 by Belitha Press
A member of Chrysalis Books plc
64 Brewery Road, London N7 9NT

Copyright © in this format Belitha Press
Series devised by Reg Cox
Design copyright © Reg Cox
Text copyright © Neil Morris
Illustrations copyright © Kevin Jones Associates

ISBN 1 84138 496 8

CIP Data for this book is available from the British Library

Printed in Hong Kong

Editor: Claire Edwards
Designed by: Cat & Mouse Design
Picture researcher: Diana Morris
Consultant: Fay Sweet

Picture acknowledgements:
Arcaid: 14 top left & 15 top right Dennis Gilbert. Architectural Association: 6 bottom left Ove Arup & Partners. Hedrich Blessing: 27 top. MacQuitty International Collection: 22 top left, 23 top left. NASA: 30 bottom, 31 top left. Quadrant Picture Library: 18 top left. Rex Features: 10 centre & 11 centre Sipa Press. Skidmore, Owings & Merrill: 26 left, 26 right Hursley. Telegraph Colour Library: 7 top left. TRH Pictures/NASA: front cover. Zefa: 19 bottom.